MW01632699

TOP
DENTISTS

"So Why Are You Getting THIS BOOK?"

That's a fair question right?

Just knowing that you have a copy of this book already tells me a lot about you. And it tells me what my friends Dr. Christian Yaste and Dr. Joe Hufanda think about you; as a patient, and as a person.

When I first began writing ***The 10 Commitments*** it was with someone like you in mind. A husband or wife, brother or sister, parent, worker, business-owner, we're all in different places in our lives, but we all have many of the same concerns, goals and challenges.

When I really began understanding what COMMITMENT was all about, I wanted to share the power of that discovery with as many people as I possibly could.

A good friend of mine who taught me much about the power of books and personal growth kept telling me I should write a "short book," only a hundred pages or so, because that's what people wanted—an easy way to read, to learn, to coach or confirm to someone special some of life's greatest lessons.

That's what you have here, a gift about life and what a powerful force commitment can be.

Commitment is stronger than motivation.
While it's certainly nice to get a "thank you" from time to time...
Giving a GIFT can be a more powerful and lasting way of showing our gratitude than just simply saying it.

So, here's your gift. A book for you...

I hope you enjoy your copy, and after you have read it, maybe you will GIFT this book to someone special in your life. It's just our way of letting you know we made a commitment a long time ago to do just a little something extra special for someone like you.

Here's to YOUR BIG LIFE!
All the best,
Michael

Several years ago at a business seminar I met Christian and Joe...

I know I probably should refer to them here as you may know them—DOCTOR Yaste and "DOCTOR" Joe.

I want you to know that they're MORE than just dentists to me. AMAZING DENTISTS (as you probably already know) sure, but even more they are friends. And over the years I've watched them grow their practice and see first-hand their commitment to becoming better in every aspect of their life; As husbands, fathers, friends, and of course, as professionals.

When we first talked of using a book as a gift for their special patients, as a sort-of "thank you" for just being you, I wanted to do something beyond just providing them this book.

So I'm writing this to let you know something you're probably already aware of—***YOU ARE SPECIAL***! There has never been and will never be anyone else quite like you. We hope reading this reminds you of that and that it might even make you smile a little bigger. Go ahead, I'm sure your dentist would approve.

Thanks for being a client of my friends Christian and Joe.
And thanks for being the kind of patient that makes them want to do a little something extra, just to say
"Hey, You're Special...and We Noticed."

Our hope is that something you'll find in these pages might just help you in some of your commitments along the way and maybe even give you a little something extra on your journey to having an amazing life.

Thank You.

For years we have tried to find an appropriate way to say "Thank You" to our patients for choosing ***Ballantyne Center for Dentistry*** as your dental care provider. Now we think we may have just found it.

We have partnered with our good friend Michael York, in order to provide you with not just a thank you gift, but also with a powerful tool to influence the direction of your life.

We hope that the words he shares in this book inspire and speak to you as much as they have to us. Too often we tend to focus only on the "*busy-ness*" of everyday, forgetting about the really important things in our lives. This book is a little reminder and should give you a glimpse into the values that we hold dear as well.

We know you could have chosen lots of other dentists to meet your specific needs. Whether you are looking for a more beautiful smile, someone who can understand your fears, a reconstruction of your "less-than-ideal" teeth, or just a healthy mouth that will last you a lifetime, we're here for you.

Our "Commitment" to you is that we and our team will do our very best to provide you with outstanding service and dental care. The kind of service and care we would provide to our own family members.

Thanks again. Be blessed.

As Michael loves to say, "Here's to YOUR BIG LIFE!"
Dr. Christian Yaste and Dr. Joseph Hufanda

The 10 Commitments

"One person with a Commitment is worth 100 who only have an interest."
–**Mary Crowley**

The 10 Commitments

First Edition, February 2005
Second Edition, June 2013

ISBN 0-9726140-2-8

Michael York
The Michael York Company, Inc.
www.michaelyork.com

Printed by
WESTMORELAND
PRINTERS
INCORPORATED
Shelby, NC

"This book is a valuable primer on the power of commitment. I was inspired and motivated by every page."

–**Jack Canfield**
Co-author, ***Chicken Soup for the Soul®***
and ***The Success Principles™***

Becoming

Thinking

Understanding

Beginning

Striving

Loving

Living

Leading

Giving

Winning

Commitment.

A strong word.

That brings powerful results.

Commitment is stronger than motivation…
and that is powerful.

"This one thing I do, forgetting those things which are behind, and reaching for those things which are before me, I press on toward the mark."

—**The Apostle Paul**

Over the years I have made many commitments.
Most of them *(especially over the past 15 years or so)* have been written down in my journals or on paper somewhere.

> *Commitment Key: Keep a written record of your commitments*

Ever wonder why a drivers license
is such a big deal?
Or why there has to be a marriage license?
A written record of a covenant between two people?
I understand some are kept today more than others, but there is a written record of that commitment none the less.

My wife and I just passed the 30 year mile marker in our commitment to one another…in marriage.
I trust you will agree with me as you read this,
that a commitment is stronger than motivation.

That means you're still committed to the "covenant" or your promise, even on the days you don't feel like it, or feel motivated to do it, or things get in a knot, as they eventually will. But your commitment means you're not basing this "thing" you've committed to on how you feel or how motivated you are today.

Commitment is stronger than motivation so we decide to keep going…*to continue.*

> *Commitment Key:*
> *Commitment is stronger than Motivation.*

In the early New Testament Church,
one of the great things that happened to the disciples and their leaders was their commitment to continue.

To keep on going.
To stay engaged in the process.
The script says they *"continued steadfastly,"*
doing what they knew they were supposed to do.
In "The Book of the Activities" *(the ACTS of the apostles),*
the commitment to their purpose is clear.
And the results were powerful.

What's your purpose?
Your mission in life?

What work are you engaged in to make a difference in the marketplace and in the lives of others?

If that doesn't sound like a job description where you work, how about a volunteer position or a "cause" that you're passionate about and could commit to advancing?

Commitment Key: Commitment is a cause and a course of action that affects your life in an uncommon way.

If you'd like to give it a try, here's some instruction and inspiration that has helped me with my commitments.

"Before you commit...
To anyone or anything,
you must first believe."

—Michael York

You must believe in something,
or there is little or no foundation to build upon.

Walt Disney once said of making dreams come true,

"When you believe in a thing,
believe in it all the way,
implicitly and unquestionably."

I have my own list of things that I believe in.
Do you have one?

If not *(or even if it's not written down),*
I encourage you to make a list.
Making a list is a powerful thing that
can begin a process.
A process that may lead you to greater achievements and incredible accomplishments…
in life and in your work.

One of my favorite lists of *"things to believe in"* comes from a book by Merrill Oster and Mike Hamel called *The Entrepreneur's Creed.*

Here's the list:

I believe in **God** as the First Principle.
I believe in the power of *dreams and visions*.
I believe in using my God-given aptitudes for *excellence.*

I believe in work as a vocation,
as *saying yes to an authentic life.*

I believe in *giving back* to build a better community.
I believe in going beyond success to *significance.*
I believe in taking calculated *risks*.
I believe in *win-win* relationships.
I believe in the value of *values*.
I believe in *lifelong learning.*

Wow.
Me too.

Do you know what you believe in?
It's the first step in making any commitment.

> *Commitment Key:*
> *Before you can commit, you must believe.*

For every individual,
motivation is a personal thing.
No one can motivate you but you.

As a professional speaker and consultant I have often heard managers or executives say…
"We need you to come out and
motivate our people!"

Sorry, can't do it.
I can't be motivational to them, and neither can you.
Why not? Simple, good questions reveal the answer.
What is motivation?

Webster says:

Inciting action, cause, inducement, purpose…CAUSING MOTION!

A reason for doing or accomplishing.

And you need a better reason than someone else telling you that you really should do this *"something."*

Understanding motivation as its defined here means one thing for certain.

There is really no such thing as a Motivational Speaker!

Unless it's you talking to you. Only you can motivate you. And that's why *self-motivation* really is the only kind of motivation.

Organizations can often spend so much time on, and so much talk on, ***"motivating"*** their workers, or members, or salespeople. When what they should be doing is spending less time "de-motivating" them.

Uncommon organizations put considerable time and energy into creating an environment that inspires and attracts talent, not only to want to be a part of that *organization, but to do whatever they must to prepare for and achieve in that role.*

It's not always easy to do, but if you think it matters, or recognize the importance of this preparation, it can become a commitment. And that's a big part of the challenge, recognizing the things that matter. Then following through or committing to them.

Inspiration on the other hand can come from an outside force. It is defined as . . .

"the act or power of arousing the mind or emotions, an agent or influence, to give inspiration to."

That's my objective as a consultant or speaker or teacher or writer, to be inspirational. To inspire or change how you think about something.
Even to change the way you think about something you already know a lot about.
About what you feel is really possible…
or impossible.

Do you realize the impossible is done everyday, somewhere?

Once upon a time, Light, Flight, The Four-Minute-Mile, and Going to the Moon, were all thought to be impossible. But now— routine.
Think about that one.

What great goal, or objective, or project, or "thing" are you working on?

Something that you may once have thought was impossible. Or maybe someone even told you it couldn't be done. That means it must be impossible, right?

Go to Disney World and look around.
Pay attention to the individuals you see,
and even those you don't see.

How do the individuals there make
The Magic Kingdom seem so magical?

What's the secret?
Somehow they make the impossible look routine almost daily.
And they make even the routine look fantastic!
There's a lesson in there somewhere for us all.

Radical improvement, high achievement, top performance and doing the impossible don't happen just because of an individual's *"motivation."*

Motivation can be temporary.
We sometimes have to do things to motivate ourselves
(I don't feel like doing this, I'm not in the mood right now...)
even when we ***say*** we really *"want"* to do the thing
we're trying to motivate ourselves toward.

But commitment is a constant.
The commitment to a vision, or cause, or goal, or thing that brings with it a personal motivation to achieve or a satisfaction from our accomplishments.

Commitment can bring about the motivation needed for an individual
to accomplish incredible things.

The drive, the pursuit, the desire to do your "thing."
Whatever that goal or cause or thing is for you.

Commitment Key:
Commitment is stronger than motivation.
Commitment is a gift you give yourself.

What inspires you?
What have you committed to?
Sadly, it seems that
most people won't do what it takes to be great, even when they know what it is... there is no lack of opportunity for greatness, only a lack of resolve.

For over FOUR DECADES now, I have pursued the clues of success and achievement as a student.

Why do some people do so well,
while the majority do not?
What I've found, just as a student who paid attention and took good notes, is that the pull of greatness or aspiring to something grand or leaving a legacy is a ***"body of work."***

It's done over time, which means it is truly a long-term goal and requires an on-going determination to not just arrive at some destination,
but to thrive and grow along the journey.
To be engaged daily in the things that really matter to you.

Constancy of purpose and the clues we can discover that have propelled others to incredible achievement or just a life of fulfillment and satisfaction...
knowing that you've made a difference in the world.

On these pages are The 10 Commitments that have been used over and over by *uncommon individuals* who achieve success at the highest level, in life and in business. These commitments are the keys to the success that many individuals say they want, or wish they had.

But wanting and wishing are common. That's why most people will go through their entire lives and never discover these clues that are so easily accessible, so readily available, to anyone who will commit to finding them and applying them.

> *Commitment Key:*
> *Many people say they wish they were someone else, or could do something other than what they're doing now. But very few people want to grow into it.*

Ever wonder why it's called "personal" development?
It's something you do for yourself, not something someone can train you to do, or something you get in a day, or a weekend, at a class or a seminar or retreat.

Oh there's instruction and inspiration in some or all of those things.
But when it comes down to your continuing improvement, the key ingredient is YOU.
What are you prepared to do with the instruction after the event has passed?
How will YOU be different, if at all?

> *Commitment Key: Top Performance and High Achievement begins with reading, listening, and writing.*

Personal Development means personal commitment to doing the things that are available and that you know you can do.

Could it really be as simple as reading, listening, and writing?

That's not a bad place for most anyone to begin.
And if you're reading this book,
you've taken the first step toward the discovery of a series of commitments that can have a major impact on how your life works out and how you enjoy living it.
If only you choose it to be so.

Reading...is confirmed by history as a clue to *top performance. Readers become leaders, create radical results, and are known as independent thinkers.*

They are more likely to be high achievers,
and lovers of life.

Yet even with the staggering evidence on the side of reading and learning as a tool for personal development and continuing improvement,
what percentage of our society would you guess actually owns a library card?

Would you believe…Less than 5%?

When I heard that statistic for the first time
I couldn't believe it.
I called the Library of Congress to ask for myself.

While they don't keep exact statistics on this issue, the projection we arrived at was somewhere between 3 and 5% of the population.

With that information in mind,
what percentage of our society would you suppose have a video-rental card?
More than 5%? Without a doubt.
In fact the number is probably closer to the 95% who don't have a library card.
Mark Twain once wrote,
"That man who doesn't read has no advantage over the man who can't read."

That's powerful instruction. Who would choose to be illiterate? Lots of individuals choose it every day, by not taking advantage of a skill many were taught as a child.

Commit to reading and exploring the pages of wisdom and knowledge and adventure and the experiences of others that add dramatically to our lives.

Commitment Key:
By choosing not to read,
you choose illiteracy and severely handicap yourself in becoming all you can be.

One thing you may notice is that each of the commitments on the list ends in I-N-G.

The reason? A reminder to us all that a commitment is *"continuing"* or on-going. It's not something ahead or something that's past it's always in the NOW, or the present tense.

"There are only two options regarding commitment;
you're either in or you're out.
There's no such thing as life in-between."
–Pat Riley, NBA Coach

Are You Ready for Commitment?

Let's Go!

The Commitment to Becoming

"Always be engaged in the process of becoming."

—Michael York

Becoming is amazing.

True success is in THE BECOMING!
And often the amazing is built on the simplest of foundations.
Some of the most amazing things in life are indeed some of the most simple. Simple pleasures, we call them.

A sunrise for example. A sunrise is a daily occurrence. Some might even refer to it as routine
(Many things in life can gradually lull us into thinking of them as routine, if only we allow it.).

Yet at times a simple sunrise is anything but.
It can be spectacular.
What must it take to become a sunrise?
Or to bring about the rising of the sun?
Only God knows for sure.

Watching a sunrise over Montego Bay
is just different than watching one
in the same place every morning.
Yet, where I grew up in rural Tennessee
remains one of my favorite places to watch the sun
come up.
Looking out the window at the horizon beyond the bean
fields where I once played as a boy.

Some might see that and say,
"What's the big deal?"

To you *(and many others)* it might seem only to be the sun coming up over a field. Something we've all seen before. But to me it is so much more.

And that is exactly how many people view making a commitment to leading a different kind of life.
To discovering what may seem so simple,
but can give such an uncommon measure of worth to an individual.

Becoming leads to many of the other commitments we will explore in this book.

Becoming Uncommon

is the name of my first book.
And what I have become as a result of the almost 10 year process it took to write it is a remarkable story.
Maybe not to everyone,
but certainly to me and to those who know me.

The goal and disciplines it took to write
270 published pages…
to think, and make notes, and pay attention, continue,
and be on the lookout for *the clues of success!*

All the while, doing my day job.
Leading me today to a place where my day job is now much different and transforming my work
in the process.

> *Commitment Key:*
> *When you want what you've never had,*
> *to become something you've never been,*
> *you must learn to do the things*
> *you've never done.*

And then make the commitment to continue doing them.
That is the key to becoming.

Today I am referred to by a different title…
Author. Consultant. Professional Speaker.

The best thing I got from that process
and those disciplines had little to do with money,
but lots to do with *THE BECOMING!*
What it made, of me.

What will "*Becoming Uncommon*"
make of you?

What would you love to do or see or have so badly that you would commit to doing almost anything it would take to achieve it?

That commitment begins the pursuit of *Becoming.*
Doesn't that sound like something worth really thinking about?

Commit to Becoming.
Becoming a husband or parent or student or whatever it is you wish to become.

*"First say to yourself what you would be;
and then do what you have to do."*
—**Epictetus**

The Commitment to Thinking

2

"Think and grow rich."

—Napoleon Hill

In *"Think and Grow Rich"* Napoleon Hill penned the secret of the ages for success in life and business. The book was first printed in 1937, and has been re-printed in over 40 editions since. One of the pages in that book contains this verse:

If you think you're beaten, you are.
If you think you dare not, you don't.
If you'd like to win, but think you can't,
It's almost certain, you won't.

If you think you'll lose, you've lost.
For out of this world we find,
Success begins with a fellow's will—
It's all in the state of mind.

If you think you're outclassed, you are.
You've got to think high to rise.
You've got to be sure of yourself before
You can ever win the prize.

Life's battles don't always go
To the stronger or faster man.
But sooner or later the man who wins
Is the one WHO THINKS HE CAN!

What do you think about?

How do you think about your life or your work or your ability to succeed?

Or do you really think at all?

A term I heard recently is "popular thinking."

Referring to the common or predominant thinking of our society today. Be on guard for *popular thinking* and where you could end up as a result.

In 1956 Earl Nightingale produced a recording called *The Strangest Secret.* It is, without a doubt, one of the most powerful messages ever recorded. Widely regarded as the beginning of the personal development (*i.e. motivational*) business boom as we know it today, it is a classic and a thought-provoking presentation you absolutely must hear someday.
In that recording, Mr. Nightingale shared the story of a young reporter asking the great doctor Albert Schweitzer,

"What is the problem with men today?"
His answer was profound.
The good doctor pondered the question for a moment and then replied,
"The problem with men today is that men simply DON'T THINK!"

Here is wisdom.
The *popular* problem with the majority of individuals *(then and now)*
is that they will allow others to think for them,
or just to tell them what they should think.

Popular thinking.
Tolerant thinking.
Politically-correct thinking.
Not thinking, or even trying.
What separates man from the rest of the species
of the earth is his ability to think.
To decide. What are you thinking about?
What have you decided? Ralph Waldo Emerson once
wrote ***"We become what we think about all day long."***

Commit to thinking.
In one ancient script, the writer described it as
a renewing process for your mind.
Without which, you'd be just like everyone else.
Common and conforming.
Be transformed.
Be renewed, by what goes into your mind
and how you use it.

I will always remember the night of the first ESPY awards broadcast on ESPN largely because of the courageous parting performance of Coach Jim Valvano.

Weakened from his battle against cancer, Jimmy V' climbed onto the platform and delivered one of the most inspirational messages I've ever witnessed.

"Three things…"
Jimmy began, gripping the podium to stand.
"Three things we should all do every day.
Laugh, be moved to tears,
and think…deeply.
Every day, don't miss a day."
What powerful advice for squeezing every drop out of life.

1. Laugh.
2. Be moved to tears (embrace your emotions).
3. And THINK…DEEEPLY!

Take some time to think.
Really think about something, anything.
Because when you only have a limited time left on this earth *(isn't that all of us),*
these are the things that really matter.
Give it some thought.

"Readers are plentiful;
thinkers are rare."

—Harriet Martineau

Commitment Key: Make time for thinking. Then capture your thoughts on paper.

Part two of this commitment is then to

CAPTURE your thoughts.

Put them on paper.
Your thoughts and ideas captured for today, and for the future.
Think, read, discuss, debate, think again, capture thoughts, and put them into action.

What could your thoughts or your ideas, become?

What could they then turn into while impacting your life or your work?
An idea or thought is just the beginning.
It's not the finished product.
Here is wisdom...

When faced with new information or new ideas

capture now...decide later.

What does that mean?
It means the in the beginning of new information or a new idea, is too soon to decide on what the long-term value might actually be to you, or your life, or your business, or your ministry. How so?

Last summer my family and I had the opportunity to see the Broadway play
The Lion King. It was stunning!
The costumes and performances were incredible.

When the idea was first suggested in 1993 to make a Broadway play from an animated movie, it was met with some resistance as you might imagine.
In fact one of the gentlemen in that meeting called it
"the worst idea in the world."

Three years later, not only did the movie become a Broadway play, but won six of the eleven Tony awards it was nominated for, and in the next 6 years would sell over 15 million TICKETS!
(Priced a ticket to a Broadway play lately?)

Not too bad for THE WORST IDEA IN THE WORLD!
The moral of the story?
Capture now. Decide later.

Everyone seems to be looking for
the answers in life.
Actually most individuals seem to be enamored with looking for the shortcut to something…to anything.
But the clues left behind for thousands of years suggest that the answers for you and I are found simply in asking better questions.

Here's one for you…

What if a greater measure of success in life was as simple as reading, listening, and writing?

(spaced repetition is a great way to learn, See p. 15)

The good news is this, that if you consider anything important and begin to do it *(really commit to it),* it will eventually become something you get enjoyment and satisfaction and pleasure and RESULTS from.

And it will most certainly transform you in the process. ***The more you read, listen, and write…the more you'll read, listen, and write.***

The popular or "common" thinking of the day is that it seems always the fault or result of some event or trend or outside condition (i.e. the day of the week, the economy, my luck, etc.) as to why an individual or an organization isn't doing better.

When the reality is that any kind of success
(or lack of it),
is an inside job and does not rest in the hands of outside forces...unless of course, you allow it to be so.

*As a man thinketh in his heart…*so is he.
How true.

"Anybody can do just about anything with himself that he really wants to and makes up his mind to do. We are capable of greater things than we realize."

—Norman Vincent Peale

One of the popular discussion topics of our day is the economy.
It has become this giant "thing"
and taken on almost a life of its own.

Talk of it creates fear and anxiety
or cause for some form of celebration.
Political and business leaders rise and fall on the popular opinion of it as polls and surveys and news channels tell each of us what we should think or feel.

Surely you'd be doing so much better if only you weren't suffering in such a "down" economy?

History confirms that in every decade and every economy over the past century there have been incredible feats of radical success
in the marketplace!

Incredible accomplishments by individuals,
dramatic and inspirational stories of success.
All have required commitment to something that is within the grasp of any individual.

Radical Growth is happening everyday… somewhere.
The Economy, while important, is but one element in the success equation of any single organization or individual. However, the clues success has left behind suggest that radical success and high achievement does not typically come from traditional *(read: out-dated*), "the-way-we've-always-done-it" kind of thinking.

It requires radical, outside-the-box, uncommon thinking. Imagination, questions, ideas, and the right attitude.
What does your attitude say about you?
It will soon tell anyone around you what you've committed to and how you think...
or don't.

While much of our society may have fallen victim to the conventional wisdom
(and I use that word only in making a point, for there is little true wisdom involved in conventional wisdom)
that says let someone else do the thinking for you or tell you what you should think and then all you as an individual will have to do is complain.

That's common right?
Ever hear someone talk about
"the common thought process?"

What if you should make a list
of all the reasons why you're not doing
better in life or business?

Then use your list to make your case?
Surely that would help your situation right?
Sadly, many people are making *(and using)*
that list right now.

Commitment Key: Are YOU on your list of why you're not doing better?

Are "you" on your list of why you're not doing better?
Make a commitment to working harder on you,
it'll pay off in a big way.

"A decision is made with the brain.
A commitment is made with the heart.
Therefore, a commitment is much deeper
and more binding than a decision."

—Nido Qubein

The Commitment to

Understanding

3

"Seek first to understand, then to be understood."

—Stephen Covey

Understanding...

Being understood.

Do you understand what a powerful position that can place us in as a communicator?

We all want to be understood,
it's the number one basic human need, even ahead of being loved…is being understood.

The next time you're involved in communicating with someone, adopt the *"you go first"* philosophy.
"Sure I want to be understood, but YOU GO FIRST!"
What if you could understand, first? Could you then become a more powerful communicator?

It's a principle that few people will actually commit to.

When practiced, it is often done in such a masterful way that it can go largely unnoticed. But it is most certainly a clue to succeeding in life and in relationships.

Relationships with husbands and wives and family and friends and customers.

Empathy. *What does it mean?*
Often we can be quick to give sympathy,
but when was the last time you sought an understanding
of others to give you empathy for that individual?
To help you truly feel what that person is feeling,
what they may be going through or trying to overcome.

Commitment Key:
Asking Begins the Understanding Process.

Asking begins the understanding process, and questions are the key. Becoming skilled at asking better questions is what true "professionals" do. Doctors, attorneys, selling professionals, parents, and countless others all must be skilled in

the art of asking better questions.

Questions are powerful, and not only are they the beginning of understanding...
they are also the key to the receiving process.
Think about it for a moment.

Here is wisdom...Ask.
And then what?
You know the rest...you shall receive!

Asking starts you on the way to your receiving.
Most people say *"I want this,"* or *"I wish I had that."*
But they never really ASK.
And I mean ask "how," as well as asking.
How could that thing happen? How could I …?

Mark Victor Hanson agrees.
"The world responds to those who ask.
Most people in this world, however,
find themselves in settled lives, never really achieving
or receiving what they hold in their dreams...
because they just never ask."
There are many good reasons to ask,
and the rewards are substantial.
If you're not moving closer to what you really want,
you probably aren't doing enough
asking."

What are common characteristics shared among
those individuals who've mastered
the art of asking?

1. Know what you want
Be clear about your vision, purpose and goals.

2. Believe that what you're asking for
is very possible.

3. Be passionate about what you're requesting.

4. Take ACTION! (even when you're afraid or feel fear)

5. Learn from experience so that you become a better "asker" with every "ask."

6. Be persistent. If at first you don't receive, keep asking!

Would you believe
You can commit to turning your life around,
no matter what challenges you may currently face?

How can you gain a clarity in what it is you really want?
How can you add passion to the process?
How can you make the leap past your feelings of fear?
If you seek…and ask…you will find!
Ask, and see what begins to happen.

What direction will you find yourself pulled in,
or propelled in?
Better questions provide the answers we're often searching for. Asking really does lead to understanding.

Commit to ASKING and UNDERSTANDING.

"The important thing is not to stop questioning."
--Albert Einstein

The Commitment to Beginning

"In the beginning, God..."

—**The Book of Genesis**

Every day is a new beginning.
Somewhere between yesterday and tomorrow is *where you are right now.*

And you have the power to choose so many things for you and your life.
Choose joy. And choose to begin the things that will bring it into your life.
Choose ... (*what would you insert here?)*
What will you choose to *begin* today?

Commitment Key:
Choose to embrace change. Change brings opportunity to you or brings you to opportunity.

Change is coming…again. It's constant.
At least it's constant around us.
But how often is change happening in us?

"There is a certain relief in change,
Though it may be from bad to worse,
as I have found in traveling in a
stagecoach; it is often a comfort to
shift one's position and
be bruised in a new place."

—**Washington Irving**

What new places have you been bruised in lately?
What have you begun to do better than ever before?
What have you begun that you've never tried before?
How are you designing and creating and planning and beginning, for the success of your life?

Beginning is preparing for whatever lies ahead. Preparing for opportunity. For when opportunity arrives, it is too late to prepare. Spectacular achievement is almost always preceded by unspectacular preparation.

Innovation is the culmination of beginning.

You don't have to be great to start something, but you do have to start something to be great.
You must begin.

Beginning leads to growing.
And growing is one of the fundamentals of life.
Growing up, growing older, growing wiser,
and growing fonder all began with...*Beginning*.
Beginning to walk, beginning school,
beginning a relationship.
Beginning a life's work or beginning to live your passion *(not just a job).*

You can even begin...AGAIN!
That's what will happen tomorrow, the day will begin... again.

"This is the day...it has been made for us,
let us rejoice and be glad in it."

Choose to be glad.
Choose to begin, everyday.
Don't just allow the days all to run together so you're never sure where you are. Or allow your attitude to be a prisoner of some outside force like those who feel bad because it's Monday or OK because it's Friday.

Be stronger than that. Choose to begin each day with an attitude that is prepared to *"seize the day."*
To grab every opportunity that may present itself today, no matter what day of the week it may be.

Shakespeare warned us that we can sometimes be our own worst enemy just by becoming too skeptical or cynical…

"Our doubts are traitors.
That make us lose the good we oft' would win, by failing to attempt."

Attempting and trying.
That is the beginning.
Begin and see what can happen for you.

Commit to BEGINNING.

"You have to find something
that you love enough
to be able to take risks, jump over
the hurdles and break through the
brick walls that are always going to be
placed in front of you.
If you don't have that kind of feeling for
what it is you're doing,
you'll stop at the first giant hurdle."

—George Lucas

The Commitment to Striving

"To strive, to seek, to find,
and not to yield."

—Tennyson

What separates us from all other creatures is our ability to strive.

"To Dream the Impossible Dream.
To Reach the Unreachable Star..."

What does it feel like to reach for something?
To go for something? To explore and to discover?
To risk and to take courage?
To press on and persist in the face of difficulty or adversity?

The definition of Striving?
"To be engaged in the process of exerting energy or effort...to struggle or contend."

Striving today seems often overcome by strife.
Life's stress can choke out our ability to strive, to change, to pursue.
It can choke the zest or passion from our life or our work or our relationships.

"What a man can wrest from truth by PASSIONATE STRIVING is utterly infinitesimal."

—Albert Einstein

Stress is a given in today's society, but we do have the ability to re-charge, to gain a fresh perspective, if only we should choose.
To "impress" upon ourselves and those around us an attitude that is *"stress-proof."*
Consider this...
Wading into a river or playing golf in the rain, the presence of water is a given.
But if you've committed to a desired condition *(staying dry),*
you'll prepare in advance for the water with waders or shoes or clothing that is "water-proof!"

This commitment and preparation will keep you in the condition of your choosing *(dry),*
in spite of the overflow of water all around you.

Stress can be overcome with commitment and preparation.
Strife can be overcome with Faith.

Faith is a partner of Striving.
You may already think you know what Faith is, but consider this…
What could you discover about Faith that you might not already know?

One Hebrew writer described Faith as,

"the substance of things hoped for, the evidence of things not seen."

Faith is substance.
And evidence.
The stuff of things hoped for.
It's there but you can't see it…yet!

If you've ever hoped for something, you were exercising your Faith and maybe you didn't even know it.
Believing that things will work out, that's Faith.

If you've ever started a new job or a new business, Faith was a part of it.
But Faith is just one part of the success formula.
There's another piece to the puzzle that says it also requires WORK.

That same writer says that Faith without WORK just doesn't make it. It's dead.
The winning formula for an amazing life requires both Faith and Work to get the greatest results.

Commitment Key: Faith!
The daring of the soul
to go farther than it can see.

Faith has an even deeper meaning to those of us who place the value of our Faith above all.

Knowing that there is a "big picture" in life that is eternal.
That's true long-term, purpose-driven, goal-setting!
Sound like something you'd like to find out more about?
Good news.
You can!

There are heroes of the Faith, those who have given their lives, or dedicated their lives to the cause of their Faith. Billy Graham would be the first name on many "*Heroes of the Faith*" list.

"Great men are they who see
that the spiritual is stronger than
any material force."

—Ralph Waldo Emerson

My personal Faith is based on a salvation that can come only one way.

From only one source.
It's based on a Biblical foundation.
And that is through a personal relationship with God, through Jesus Christ.

If you'd prefer to skip this part, that's your choice as the reader.

Skipping and skimming information to the part you need most is part of becoming a good student.

The fact that you may not believe as I do will not offend me. I may be saddened.
Or challenged, but not offended. And I do not write this to offend you. But to fulfill one of my commitments, to be a witness and an influence for a cause.

If in fact this is a message that you need or you'd like to know more about,
then it's here for you.

I tell many of my live audiences the sad truth is that ***not everyone will "get" the message of the day.***
Whether becoming uncommon, personal development or business development, even spiritual development, not everyone gets the message.
For any number of reasons.

But those who do get it,
will most assuredly have a better life and work and purpose than those who don't.
No matter what life holds in store.

That's especially true when it comes to this kind of information…this spiritual information.

At a recent Peter Lowe Success Event, with 20,000 people who had paid to be in attendance, Peter referred to a survey his organization had done on what "you the attendee" wanted to see more of in these type of events.

The 2 most prominent and prevailing messages you wanted were *more Financial lessons and more Spiritual sessions.*

And more "purpose-driven" messengers delivering those sessions.

Zig Ziglar, Peter Lowe, Jim Rohn, and many more hi-profile, hi-purpose, believers neither apologize for, nor hide the fact that they are Christians.

Very cool.

As a good student I have chosen to follow their examples.

And to follow His example. I am a follower of Christ.

> *Commitment Key: Once you've made a commitment, there will come a time for you to take a stand.*

The Bible says there is but one way to come to the Father,

and that is Jesus the Christ.

I know that's not the most popular message of the day, but there will come a time if you have made a commitment, for you to take a stand.
To go beyond compromise, even when it is called by names like tolerance or religious teachings of good men.

To stand with resolve upon the foundation of your beliefs.

To stand upon the principles of Truth,
and the wisdom of generations before us.
Times that call for you to draw a line in the sand,
even if the wisdom of the day deems it unpopular.
If we're a good student in this area we will come to certain conclusions that are irrefutable!
That means they are Truth.

And Truth is under attack at every turn
in our world today.

"The Bible is a great business tool because the principles it teaches don't change.

Technology and marketing dynamics change almost daily...

but God's wisdom on how to treat people doesn't change."

–Don Cathy, Senior VP
Chick-fil-A

Zig Ziglar's response to those who *"may not be quite as enthusiastic as I am about the value of Biblical advise,"* the dynamic platform speaker says as his southern drawl crawls into a smile...

"I encourage you to remember this,

According to a recent issue of Fortune magazine, 91% of the (leaders) of Fortune 500 companies... learned their values, ethics, and morals from the same source—

the Bible and the Church.

At least they claimed an affiliation...

and less than 7% said they had no *(form of Faith).*"

Zig continues,

"If W. Edwards Deming, Tom Peters, Warren Bennis, or Fred Smith had written a book that had positively affected the lives of 91% of the leaders of Fortune 500 companies, how many of you would head for the bookstore and get yourself a copy?"

There is a certainty in *"the facts."*

And an even greater certainty as the collection of facts increases over time. History confirms that some things are too obvious to deny.

The sunrise we read of earlier for example, no one can "*deny the dawn.*" It is too obvious!

The sun will come up AGAIN tomorrow.
For a time or a season, someone could argue against it—but eventually the obvious is confirmed.
And so it will be with Faith, and Heaven, and Salvation, the Bible and Jesus Christ…too obvious to deny.

And, one day, too late to change one's mind.
In the words of a passing car's bumper sticker,

"If you're living like there is NO GOD—
You'd better be right!"

"Most people spend more time at work than anywhere else...

People are no longer satisfied to compartmentalize their faith life from their work life. They want to be the same person 7 days a week.

They don't want to leave their souls in the company parking lot."

–David Miller, former IBM executive

Striving is pressing on "toward the mark," as one inspired writer put it.

Having the goal in sight and not losing focus in the pursuit of that goal or target.

Do you have a target?
Do you have a goal?
Probably not. I mean either you have no goal *(written down),* or you have ***goals, plural.***
More than one.
The clues of success say it's tough to have just one goal.

When you know the power of goals, having them and reaching them, chances are good that you will have more than one.

You may have one overriding goal or mission or purpose or objective,

but as a student I've found people who set goals have a whole list of things that are important to them. Things written down that they are in the pursuit of.

"What would life be if we had no courage to attempt anything?"

—Vincent Van Gogh

It's really easy to strive for a goal.

Take a few minutes and think about what it is you want.

What you want to do or be or have or give or be known for…and then write it down.

Now you've got *written goals.*

Keep them nearby and look at them on a regular, if not daily, basis. You'll begin to feel the power and the pull and the energy that having a written goal can provide.

And striving toward that goal gives you a purpose.

A cause or a reason for doing things, just in case you begin asking yourself one day,

"Why am I doing this?"

You'll know. You're striving.

For a goal or cause or reason or purpose.

"There is a problem with even a
little bit of neglect.
Neglect starts as an infection.
If you don't take care of it,
it becomes a disease. And one (area of)
neglect leads to another.
Worst of all, when neglect starts,
it diminishes our self-worth.

Once this has happened,
how can you regain your self-respect?
All you have to do is act now!
Start with the smallest discipline that
corresponds to your own philosophy.
Make the commitment:

I will discipline myself to achieve my goals so that in the years ahead I can celebrate my successes."

—Jim Rohn

Commit to STRIVING!

The Commitment to Loving

"How far you go in life depends on you being tender with the young, compassionate with the aged, sympathetic with the striving and tolerant of the weak and the strong. Because someday in life you will have been all of these."

—**George Washington Carver**

Love never fails.
It's the greatest.
It's a powerful thing to commit to loving anything.

Like a child. Or your husband, or wife.
Or just life itself.

I mean really *"in love with"* someone or something.
Being passionate!
With a zest, or a zeal, being truly committed to that *"thing."*

What is Love?

There are unfortunately generations of people today who mistakenly define it in the same way as lust or sex or worse. But that's not love. Love is devotion and dedication and compassion and sometimes it's not an enjoyable experience at all.

Have you ever done something to hurt someone who loves you and you know they still love you even after you've hurt them or disappointed them?

That's gaining an understanding of what love is, and what loving does.
Loving serves and supports and encourages and understands…or tries to, even in the face of disappointment and frustration.

Love disciplines because it desires a different outcome than the undisciplined behavior produces.

Love is patient. Love is kind.
Easy to say… Easy to read.

Often hard to live out in our daily lives.
Loving is a commitment, a devotion or a duty.
And as LOVE…I-N-G it is on-going and continuing.
In the present tense.

Love of God and Country
have sent many a brave soldier to face death
or pay the ultimate price by laying down their life.

Love is courageous.
Love suffers long.
And Love never fails. The evidence supports it.
History confirms it.

Commitment Key: Don't neglect expressing your love to those around you.

It's sad how often we express our love casually…
Or sometimes not at all until it's too late.
If you had to write down a few words to describe how you feel about your spouse, or your child,
or your father or mother…what would you write?

When you send a card do you write your feelings in it?
Or do you just depend on the writer of the card?
Would you rather get just a signed card,
or a card with a hand-written and heart-felt few words from someone who took the time to
tell you how they really feel about you?

In my book, *"Becoming Uncommon"* I share several passages from my personal journals on very private times with my family and friends.

Personal development is, well…personal.
And I've included those entries so that you can understand the power of words in conveying your love for someone or something.

Don't say you can't do it,
because you can…if only you will.
Say you won't try it, but don't say you can't do it.
If you sit down and look at a photo album,
or you think of childhood memories, or being a
newlywed, or whatever; the words will come to you.

It may seem awkward at first, but love deserves you making the attempt. Don't wait till you can do it well.
Anything worth doing is worth doing POORLY,
until you can do it well.
The rewards are amazing, give it a try.

"Greater love hath no man…"
Commit to LOVING.

"Anyone can dabble,
but once you've made that commitment,
your blood has that particular thing in it,
and it's very hard
for other people to stop you."

—Bill Cosby

The Commitment to Living

"I dream for a living."

—Steven Spielberg

Don't trade living for existing.

Living and Loving

are an unbeatable combination.

I love hearing one of my teachers for over 25 years, talk about how he spends each day with his *"redhead"* and how he loves her more today than ever.
Love stories are compelling. Life stories are inspiring.

Love + Life = Living

I mean really getting the most out of every day, because that's what you've chosen.

To squeeze every drop from all the experiences you face today. To take all your life experiences over all your years, gather them up and invest them into today…
in an effort to get the greatest return for your life!
That's living. And it is most certainly an uncommon way of looking at life.

How many people do you know that struggle through each day, just like the one before…
uninspired, complaining, discouraged, grumpy,
how disappointing.

They say they're disappointed
in how their life's worked out.
What if…life were likewise disappointed in
what these individuals have settled for?

And if you're still breathing, life's not over yet!
What is it about your life that you
ABSOLUTELY LOVE?

What would you like to change about your life?
About your work? About your legacy?
It's available!

If only you're available…
That's the real question.
All you have to do is to choose…
and then decide what you will do to change your life!
Let the living begin.
All over again.

Living is like that.

Unfortunately only a very small percentage of our society will ever make that choice,
to really live their lives…
instead of just settling for some mundane existence.
Sad, but true.

"Dost thou love life?
Then do not squander time,
for that is the stuff that life is made of."

—Ben Franklin

How are you investing your time to get the most from your life?
To gain an enjoyment or fulfillment that few people will ever know. Sadly many will say
"I don't have the time to read," or study, or laugh,
or whatever.

But here are the facts…

They all have exactly the same amount of time as anyone who's wealthy, or special, or exceptional,
or successful. ***And so do you!***
The maximum amount of time allowed by law…
24 hours a day, 7 days a week!
And that's all there is as far as we know, you couldn't get anymore if you tried. And most people aren't trying, they're just complaining.

That's 168 hours in a week.

Wow. What are you doing with all that time?
How are you investing it for the greatest return on life?

To find out truthfully, how much time
you spend watching TV…
and how much time you spend reading, or praying,
or playing with your kids?

Try keeping a journal on your time and where you
spend it (or invest it) for one week.
It's eye-opening!
Some clichés are true,
like all work and no play making you dull.
But some are subtle deception, like time is money.
Not true.
Time is so much more. If you lose all your money,
there will be time and opportunity for more to be made.
But losing your time with children or family or loved
ones cannot be recaptured or bought back at any price.

Lots of things that scream for our attention seem urgent.
Seldom does urgency carry the badge of importance.

Commitment Key: There are very important things that can go unnoticed unless you're really paying attention to LIVING your life.

There are very important things that can often go
unnoticed unless you're really paying attention to
LIVING your life.

As you consider many of the commitments in this book,
you may begin to add new commitments along the way.

I've even added another commitment at the end of this book.

It's a bonus commitment just for you.
How amazing that the "law of inertia" really does work!
How is it that once you begin, you find more than you thought was there or more than you imagined could be?

"There's more to see than can ever be seen, more to do than can ever be done."
--**Elton John,** *The Circle of Life*

A few commitments beget a few more.
A handful of small disciplines lead to greater ones.
Being faithful in small things leads to greater rewards and accomplishments.

It's ancient wisdom. And wisdom is something all good students should pay careful attention to,
in your pursuit of the Truth in life.
Wisdom is more than just knowledge and has much to say on Truth, and life, and living it.

And if you're a diligent student of life, and ancient wisdom, you'll eventually discover that life can be longer than you may have ever imagined…
It's a life that's referred to in the Bible as *"eternal."*

Doesn't that sound like something we would have to look into?

Make a commitment to LIVING and LIFE,
not just existing or going through the motions
day after day.

While you're at it, become a good student of "spiritual life" and find out how long your life could actually be.

"How different our lives are
when we really know what is
deeply important to us,
and keeping that picture in mind,
we manage ourselves each day
to be and to do
what really matters most."

—Stephen Covey

The Commitment to Leading

*"He who is firm in will,
molds the world to himself."*

—Von Goethe

What's the first thing that comes to mind when I ask you to make a commitment *to Leading?*

Leadership?

Think of leading as the opposite of following.

If we're cutting a path through the jungle, or the new world, or the new economy,
and there's thick growth on all sides, lots of congestion,
it's often hard to see where we're going.
Maybe we're in single file…one behind the other.

Each one is leading the next.
Think about this...
The only person leading you
is the one directly in front of you.
Not necessarily the person who is 7, or 8, or 10 persons ahead of you.

You have your head down, working hard to make it through, and keeping in sight or at the very least close contact with, the person in front of you.
That person is *leading* you.
And you are *leading* the person behind you.

Leading is something we should think of on a very individual or personal basis.
You can have an effect on someone, and how their life works out, even if you wouldn't necessarily consider yourself a leader.

Could you be a leader? Could you be *leading* others? Influencing them in a certain direction?
And the answer is absolutely.
Someone is watching your "leadership" skills right now. If you were in that single file line moving through the jungle, you not only could be, but you WOULD be, a leader. Maybe even without realizing it.

That is exactly what is happening today in our world. People are leading without realizing, other people are then following without realizing it, and often neither really knows where they are going.
As a result, they both are lost.

They have no idea the direction they're heading.
But lots of other people are going in that direction,
so it must be OK. Right?

Commitment Key: Understand that "Leading" doesn't really take any courage at all.

Leading doesn't really take any courage at all in spite of what you may have heard or read. People are being led down the wrong path every day in life, or work, or...

and they think they're doing the right thing.

But leadership, true leadership, is different.
Finding your own path, going against the grain may not be popular, but if you're in the smaller percentage group of top performers, high achievers, believers, etc. you're leading...EVEN IF NO ONE APPEARS TO BE FOLLOWING YOU!

True leaders don't produce more followers, they strive to produce more leaders.
Leaders who are leading and know where they are going, even if no one is following them ***at the moment.*** Being different or independent means standing for something you believe in and have committed to, even if you must stand alone...for now. Somewhere, someone is waiting to join you, waiting for a leader.

In the beginning, the crowd is seldom right.

Popular thinking typically produces
unpopular results…History confirms it.
Great minds don't think alike.
Great minds have proven to be independent thinkers.
General Patton once said

"If everyone's thinking alike,
then someone's not thinking."

How true.

And leading requires both thinking and understanding. How sad that generations of our young people say they want to be different, do their own "thing" and become independent.

But their actions say they want to fit in
and be like a certain group or crowd or peer.
That's conforming, to peer pressure.

Commitment Key: True Leadership can't be about everyone liking you or some popularity contest.

Leadership can't be about everyone liking you or some popularity contest. That's why true leaders create polar reactions and spur hotly-contested debates.
For them, and what they stand for…or against them.

Uncommon leaders have staked out a position that cannot always be a popular one, and they will not change their position just to gain popularity.

It doesn't mean being close-minded or stubborn,
but being convinced and committed if you believe it to be the right position.
Having values, morals, integrity, principles of conviction, and standing on them.
Be a good student.
Then become a committed leader.
The crowd may come around later.

There are many "common" misconceptions on leaders and leadership.

Phil Knight of NIKE once remarked that,
THERE IS ONLY ONE LEADER!
That sounds powerful…ONLY ONE!
Black & white, win or lose,
no room for finishing second…

Webster defines leadership as
"the ability or capacity to lead."

Just above that entry in the new college dictionary under the word "leader" there are more than 13 references or definitions of "LEADER."

And really not one of those definitions I found were appropriate in delivering a message to a group of individuals or to an organization that wants to truly understand leaders and genuine leadership.

I was disappointed in that discovery,
but just a few entries down that same page was the definition of LEADING EDGE…

"the edge of a sail or vessel that faces the wind. The vanguard; the beginning or lead position in a movement."

The Leading Edge…
That was the picture I was looking for.

The setting of the sail, the direction we've chosen to go, the point at which we face the challenge and adversity ahead…the winds of change, and that leading edge of individual or group that propels us through it…

Does that give you a mental picture?

It's not a bad definition of how true leaders meet the challenge of leadership.

And true leaders can be anywhere in the organization, not just at the top.

"The key to transforming yourself from someone who understands leadership to a person who successfully leads in the real world is CHARACTER. Your character qualities activate and empower your leadership ability— or stand in the way of your success."

— John Maxwell, The 21 Indispensable Qualities of a Leader

Could character really have an impact on leading?

And the answer is without a doubt.
Dr. Maxwell goes on to say in his book that
"leaders cannot rise above the LIMITATIONS OF THEIR CHARACTER!"

Did you realize that your character
could actually limit you,
or help advance you as a leader?

Honesty and Integrity are qualities we find in most all true leaders. Leading does reflect many of the leadership qualities that we've always heard about… vision, powerful communication, etc.
There's more to leading than first meets the eye.
It's true that leaders can have a powerful influence on others…but so can losers!

Leadership is mostly about influence.
If you hang around with the wrong crowd they will soon lead you into the jungle, having their own *"influence"* on you, though they would seldom be described by their actions as a "leader."
Having Influence is something that happens by association.

If you and I spend major time together,
only one of two things can happen;
Either you will become more like me,
or I will become "influenced" to be more like you.

But as a *"leading edge"* individual, you can stay on your path, headed toward your life target, in spite of the influence others may try and exert on YOU.

In a survey on the most-desired characteristics and qualities of leadership, a long list of things was presented to the respondents on what we truly wanted in our leaders.

Here's the list...

Ambitious
Caring
Competent
Cooperative
Courageous
Dependable
Determined
Fair-minded
Forward-looking
Honest
Imaginative
Inspiring
Intelligent
Loyal
Mature
Self-controlled
Supportive
Straight-forward

The number one quality?

Honesty!

88% said they wanted their leaders to be honest.
Just tell the truth. Be someone who can be trusted.

> *Commitment Key:*
> *The most desired quality in a leader is HONESTY! Become Trustworthy.*

My friend, anyone is capable of that leadership quality. Once upon a time, that was a common value, now seemingly all too rare. Reserved it seems, only for leaders.

The other qualities?

- 71% said they wanted someone who was "forward-looking," a visionary. Someone who could look beyond today and the short-term, and see the excitement and promise of the future.

- 66% said a leader should be COMPETENT. Seems it's a good thing to know a little about what you're doing. To keep up the learning curve and not just depend on experience, since the marketplace and life is always growing and changing.

- And, 65% said they wanted a leader who was INSPIRING!

Inspiring?
That's not really necessary now is it?
How about just some training, just the facts.
Wouldn't that be enough?
While so many individuals are consumed or concerned about things that don't really matter in the big picture of life, what we should be concerned about is being "un-inspired."

Inspiration is powerful. It's fuel and fire and energy that moves us to action. And individuals who are honest and competent, with the ability to inspire others and propel them into a brighter future will most certainly become leaders. Or already are.

Commit to LEADING.

"Be strong and courageous…
that thou may prosper wherever you go."
—Joshua 1:7

The Commitment to

Giving

"Give and it shall be given unto you. Pressed down, shaken together, running over..."

–The Bible

Giving and serving.

These two qualities go together. Hand and glove.
This could just as easily be the commitment to serving.
Being "at the service" of someone or something.
Giving of your time or your talents or your funds toward a cause, or group, or individual.

Did you realize that you can give something away and it can result in you getting more of it yourself?

It's called *encouragement.*

It means literally *"to put courage inside."*
And you have the power to give away courage to someone else and encourage yourself in the process.

When you instruct or encourage others it gives you the chance to say it again and again.
It's encouraging to hear, for them and for you.
And each time you do it, you hear it again.
That individual may be hearing it only once,
but you get to hear it over and over and over.
Take courage. And give courage away.

Someone you know needs to be encouraged today.
It could take only a few moments of your time,
but will have a lasting impact on that individual.

Commitment Key:
Giving makes you bigger than you are.

Giving makes you bigger than you are.
The more you give, the more you pour out,
the more life will be able to pour into you.

The book of The Activities in the New Testament speaks over and over of the disciples being *"filled."*
It wasn't because they didn't get it the first time,
or they spilled it, but because they poured themselves
into life and into their work.
They gave it all they had and there came a time when they needed to re-fuel. To re-fill.

That time comes for all of us.
Unfortunately many people keep right on going, not slowing down or stopping for a fresh filling. It might be time off from a job or work. It could be a filling or a refreshing that just allows some family time, or quiet time, or time with a good book…maybe **The** Good Book.

We all need another filling. When's your next filling? Where's your filling station?
How are you pouring yourself out?
For what purpose or cause?
How are you sharing or giving to enrich your life and the lives of those around you?

I recently returned from 16 days in Africa.
Over those 16 days and the days that followed, I almost filled a journal with notes on my thoughts and experiences there.

> ***"What an adventure it has been. A roller coaster of experiences and emotions, from exhilaration to exhaustion, things exciting and things tragic… It has been a trip that expands the mind and the heart, and compels one toward understanding and compassion.***
>
> ***The conditions are in many cases, indescribable- even unthinkable, but the people here don't complain, or even seem to notice. They just press on…What a great lesson in both appreciation for life and the perseverance to continue in it."***

There is so much we can give that would be so easy to do from our bounty of whatever we have.
And I don't just mean financially.
Giving to a cause or a movement that we feel strongly about.
Webster defines MISSIONARY as
"one sent or engaged in the activities of a mission."
What's your mission?
What are you engaged in that could make a difference in how a life works out?
What cause are you giving to with your time and your service?

I've heard many well-meaning individuals talk about giving to God.
But I've never heard a lesson on giving any more powerful than from Charlie "Tremendous" Jones (author of *Life is Tremendous*), when he asked the question...

"What in the world could you give to the God of the universe?"

How can you give something back to someone who created it all in the first place?
What if we would only "return" something of value to show our thanks?
Return thanks. Return a portion of what we have, to God and His work.
We can give to men and women and children and family *(and we should),* but we can only **return** to God as good stewards, a portion of that which we have been blessed with.

And it may not just be financially.
In fact it should be so much more than just money.
Our time, our work, our mission or purpose in life,
our legacy; all are things that require us to give…
and it's given back to us, in return.
As one script records it, *"pressed down, shaken together, and running over."*

Now I should mention much of the work that gets done here on this earth will require money from somewhere. It's going to cost a lot of shillings to build that orphanage in Kenya.

And to educate doctors and send missionaries
and build schools, money will be required.
To help friends who are out of work…
and the list goes on.

Let us give "cheerfully"
whatever it is we have to give.

Commitment Key: Become a Cheerful Giver

At least once each year we celebrate Thanksgiving…
giving thanks for what we have.

What are you thankful for?
What have you been given?
And how do you measure what you have?

Try measuring your worth not in dollars or possessions, but the things in your life for which you would not take money.
Priceless things…not for sale at any price.

Things that you would still have and still want,
even if you suddenly found yourself out of work,
or your possessions all went away,
or your lifestyle dramatically changed.

"No person was ever honored
for what he received,
honor is the reward for what he gave."

—Calvin Coolidge

10 The Commitment to Winning

"You must be single-minded. Drive for one thing on which you have decided."
-- George S. Patton

Character, Honesty, and Intcgrity play an equally important role in winning, as in leading.

If you think about it, it only makes sense
when you consider that most often winning means at some point you must be "leading."
For just a moment, I'd like you to think a bit differently about that word. *Winning*.
How would you answer this question...

How many winners in a race?
When I ask that question to live audiences,
the answer is most often the same.
One.
That's it, just one.
But how many winners in a MARATHON?

Many? All who run?
Whatever your answer, chances are it's more than just one. And that's what's available to you in life.
Not that if someone else wins, it means you have to lose.

That if someone else has a lot *(of anything)*
that must then leave less for you.
It's just not true.
The law of abundance says
there's plenty to go around.

Plenty, of anything for you and me.
If we really want it.

The next lesson is this,
you don't just "show up" to run a marathon.
26.2 miles? You can't just decide today
that you can win tomorrow.
Or even compete.

About how far would you expect you'd get?
Nope, there's got to be a little more planning and preparation than that to even be in the "running."

When opportunity arrives
it is too late for preparation.

Prepare for winning.
It is a major key.
And winning isn't just for games either…
how about winning the battle?
The battle for your time or the battle for your mind?
Or the battle for the mind of your children?

Who is winning that one? How are you contributing to the development of young minds?

> *Commitment Key:*
> *When opportunity arrives it is too late for preparation.*

Winning is daily.
It is I-N-G!
It is a commitment and something that must occur on a consistent basis.
Only if that's really what you've chosen.

Winning is terrific. A winner is someone we're attracted to. It's someone we want to be, and we can.
What comes to mind if I say "Olympic Champion?"
A winner?
An athlete?
Gold medals?

The real story of any Olympic champion is much more than the race or the event and medals and national anthems. It's what went on before, or even during the "becoming" of a champion that is such a testament to winning and overcoming.

Preparation, daily discipline, attitude, commitment, perseverance, the list is a long and familiar one.

At least the words are familiar, but the execution of all those things is extraordinary.
And the results bear that out.
The spoils of victory seem like so much fun,
so pleasurable…
but almost no one wants to hear how the winner got there. Especially if the message means wanting you to do the same. To prepare or develop disciplines or improve your attitude.

Are you prepared to do what it takes to
duplicate that kind of winning?

Commitment Key:
In Life, or in most any competition,
the Winning is in the Becoming.

In life, or in most any competition,
the winning is in the becoming. And the commitment to continue doing the things you know you must do,
even when you'd rather not do them.

For any champion, the story is much the same.
All the hours of work and preparation and sacrifice;
There must be an easier way, right?

Know anyone who thinks like this?
You might be amazed at the vast numbers of people looking for a short-cut to winning in life.

"If I ever win the lottery..." How sad.
They're looking for a short-cut to everything, and all too often what appears to be a short cut turns into a detour.

A wrong turn that takes an individual from the path of success or path of destiny that has been prepared specifically for you if only you'd stay the course.
Press on toward the mark.

"One of the most dangerous aspects of contemporary living is short-term thinking."

—**Rick Warren**, *The Purpose-Driven Life*

One of the subtle deceptions in this life is to chase financial rewards at any cost.
Money-motivated is the myth.
Taking your eyes off the real prize of life and living to pursue gold, money, things, stuff…
instead of fighting the good fight?

Instead of committing to the daily disciplines that can lead us to a greater measure of success in life.

Money is something we attract by the person we become. Or the value we bring to the marketplace. It is not the finish line or the prize worthy of all our time, energy and efforts. Not something to exchange the pieces of our lives for that are of the greatest worth, that money cannot buy.

You see them everyday.
Individuals who've chosen not to prepare for the journey, chosen not to place much stock in the *"winning"* attitudes and habits and work ethics. Chosen to short-change or ignore the important things and people around them to cash in on the big payday.

"If you only knew how special you are right now in the eyes of a child."
--Michael York

If you'll only pay attention on your way through the jungle, you'll know these are not the people you want to be following.

Be a good student and discover what winning is really all about in life.
Even if you don't finish first…
Commit to WINNING.
And then prepare for your opportunity.

As you begin new disciplines, you will develop more disciplines in the process.

It's the power of inertia that keeps you in motion toward your goal or objective.
Inertia is a law that can work for you or against you, and just by beginning any task,
no matter how difficult, you are propelled in the direction of completing that task!
Give it a try and see how it works for you.

"The longer I live, the more I am certain that the great difference between the great and the insignificant, is energy – invincible determination – a purpose once fixed and then death or victory."

—Sir Thomas Buxton

1 The Commitments yet to come…

"I have fought a good fight.
I have finished my course.
I have kept the faith."

— 2 Timothy 4:7

Finding your purpose in this life is powerful.

Commit to it and it will reward you in so many wonderful ways, many of which will be unique to you and you alone.

After the lion's share of this manuscript was completed,

and long after the Original 10 Commitments
had been uncovered,
I came across a new commitment
that was so important that I actually went back
and wrestled with dropping one of the 10 originals
so I could add this new discovery.

But I couldn't find one that could be replaced.
The original 10 had to remain intact.
And so, as the model set thousands of years ago…
and as an added bonus from a committed student,

a NEW COMMITMENT I give to you.

A commitment that as you pursue your life and your work and your purpose and your faith,
you will not forget to practice this "new" commitment…

Practice Slowing.
In fact, Commit to it.
My goal?
*"To ruthlessly eliminate hurry
from my life!"*

What exactly does that mean?

I've heard countless times from individuals who've had a tragedy or health issues or something traumatic happen in their lives and it caused them to take stock of what's really important. And what's really important is LIFE. And living it to the fullest.

Not rushing on things that in the long run aren't really important at all.

From time to time, slow down.
Whatever you happen to be in pursuit of at the time, know when to dial it down and when to pour it on.
When to drink it in and when to fill your glass.
There is a difference between
"rushing" and a *"sense of urgency"* when completing a task or project.

Results are necessary, from work and from life.
Rushing isn't.
Refresh.
Renew.
Recharge.
Slow down. Enjoy.

Life Key: Practice slowing...

Practice slowing.

Bet that's not something you've heard lately at any company meeting or motivational seminar, huh?
S-L-O-W-I-N-G.
Do we even know what that feels like anymore?

I was just reading an email message from a "training" organization and the line that really struck me was…

"The end of March is here as well as the end of the first quarter of this year. Have you accomplished your first quarter goals?
If not, and life has gotten in the way..."
If Life has gotten in the way?

Stuff gets in the way...Life is what allows us to still be here to deal with the stuff...
to achieve goals, pursue our purpose, and do whatever else we're engaged in.
Life does not get in the way, that's miscommunication and a lack of understanding.
The real problem is that most people are not engaged in the process of Life.
The paradox is there's a lack of energy, and at the same time too much energy expended on the day-to-day "stuff" and not enough expended on Engaging Life.
Hey, let's do some Life today!
Goals are great,
but lets hope Life never stops getting in the way.

How are you living your Life?
With purpose?
With meaning?
With energy and attitude? What attitude have you CHOSEN to face today with?
Have you found your "thing"
that makes Life worth living?
A relationship or a cause or a reason for being?

Don't treat Life like it's just getting in the way.
Like all the day-to-day stuff is keeping you from fulfilling your dreams,
or purpose, or goals…

Celebrate Life!
Don't be like all those people who put off living for someday, somewhere in the distant future.

"One day," they tell themselves,
"When I pay off this or that,
when I put back enough money...
when I retire, I shall live happily ever after."
When exactly is that day?
Have you circled it on your calendar?

Life doesn't offer many sure things beyond today.
And the truth is there's no station to arrive at once and for all, the great thing about Life is the journey.
The LIVING!

If you'd like to "re-think" your Life and your goals, here are a few suggestions.

I'm sure you can come up with a few more on your own if you'll just begin the process.

Slowly, now…

1. Set Goals for your Life, not just Work

What's your goal for your life?

Your plan or your purpose?

What's really important to you along the way?

Life's answers begin with great questions you ask yourself. Most people who have any written goals at all, have them only for their work. *(Usually sales goals)*

2. Treat work as a Project.

That means a beginning and an ending. A place to know when you're finished so you can celebrate the achievement or re-charge for the next project. If all your work seems to flow as a constant with no discernable beginning or ending, try making it a monthly or quarterly "window" of time.

3. Don't be a Martyr for the Company.

Take a vacation. A long weekend is OK,
but 7 or 8 days is better.

Make time to de-compress and un-wind.

Some clichés are true, like *"all work and no play"* making you dull. Some aren't true, like *"Time is Money."*

Time is so much more than that, and once it's gone it can't be bought or replaced.

Long hours aren't the best measure of performance or results. There are times to pour it on, but that can't be a constant. Even NASCAR's professional drivers know the danger of hitting the wall, and the need for "slowing" once in a while.

4. Time-Management is the Wrong Objective.

Time is oblivious to anything you or I can do to harness it. It rolls on. Better objective is ME-management, understanding the difference between investing time in something valuable and important, or just spending time creating no real lasting value.

5. Don't be so Serious.

Life is short, loosen up. Try laughing once in awhile, or getting away for an afternoon to do something you enjoy. A survey of top performers showed they spent 8-10 hours each week on recreation…or at least they said they did. Even if it's not every week try "re-creating" your enjoyment for living periodically.
People around you will notice…and so will you.

6. Simplify.

Make your life and work, and the lives and work of those around you, EASIER. Don't ask me how, if you seek you will find. It's ancient wisdom.

7. Don't neglect Celebration.

Celebration is the candle on the cake of Life.

Don't let anything blow yours out.

Life is big.

Live it that way.

Why not start today?

Practice Slowing.
It's the new commitment for "Now."

"The World is round and the place which
may seem like the end,
can actually be the beginning."
—Ivy Baker Priest

Welcome to
"The Beginning of Becoming!"

A Gift For You…

Download Michael's E-Books and more FREE STUFF on Facebook at :

Michael York's COOL SCHOOL

The NOW Economy:
Cool Rules & Tools for Winning Today!

My Greatest Lessons:
How to Design & Live an Amazing Life!
(Coming in 2014 !)

Michael York
Student & CEO

Michael York wrote the book on
"Becoming Uncommon!"

He's been called
*"a unique and entertaining teacher
who makes learning fun,
beats boring training, and helps
individuals and organizations to
become more powerful than the status-quo."*

As a consultant, he is the "Chief Learning Officer" for many different companies and organizations on thinking differently and creating radical results.

As a businessman, he is the founder and CEO of The Michael York Company, Inc. in Charlotte, North Carolina. Beginning his career in direct sales in 1978, Michael now has over 35 years of sales, marketing, and management experience.

He has spoken live to thousands of audiences across the country, and around the world. On subjects that range from personal development to powerful communication to winning in any economy.

He has been on speaking platforms from the MGM Grand in Las Vegas, to Washington DC, to Walt Disney World… addressing business leaders from cruise ships in the Bahamas, to downtown hotels in Nairobi, Kenya.

In 2002 he launched ***COOL $chool***, and The Michael York Learning Center, to provide continuing improvement in sales and business training systems; live and on video, for business owners, selling professionals and association members.

Michael's columns have appeared in national publications and online across the country and around the world, as well as in his monthly E-Magazine, ***"Becoming Uncommon."*** ***Read his columns regularly online at*** ***www.MeincMagazine.com and*** ***www.TheNetworkMarketingMagazine.com among many others.***

To subscribe or for more information on Michael York go to *www.michaelyork.com*

For speaking inquiries or products, email *leader@michaelyork.com*

"You Can't Change People.
But if you can change their minds,
change the way they think;
People will change themselves."

—Michael York

Michael York